The Presbyterian Elder

The Presbyterian Elder

Paul S. Wright
Revised by W. Ben Lane

The Westminster Press
Philadelphia

First published as *The Duties of the Ruling Elder,* copyright 1957 by W. L. Jenkins; copyright © 1972 The Westminster Press

© 1986 The Westminster Press

Scripture quotations are from the Revised Standard Version of the Bible, copyrighted 1946, 1952, © 1971, 1973 by the Division of Christian Education of the National Council of the Churches of Christ in the U.S.A., and are used by permission.

Book design by Christine Schueler

First edition

Published by The Westminster Press®
Philadelphia, Pennsylvania

PRINTED IN THE UNITED STATES OF AMERICA
9 8 7 6 5 4 3 2 1

Library of Congress Cataloging-in-Publication Data

Wright, Paul S.
  The Presbyterian elder.

  Rev. ed. of: The duties of the ruling elder.
Rev. ed. 1972.
    1. Presbyterian Church—Government. 2. Elders
(Church officers) I. Lane, W. Ben. II. Wright,
Paul S. Duties of the ruling elder. III. Title.
BX9195.W7 1986   262'.15   86-1603
ISBN 0-664-24014-3 (pbk.)

Contents

Contents

Introduction

If you are reading this book, you probably have been elected an elder by your congregation. It may have been given to you as part of a program of training and development in which you will be involved before you are ordained by the session and installed as an active member of that session. When you were asked if your name might be placed in nomination for the office of elder, you doubtless had some doubts and questions: Am I the right person? What is an elder and what do elders do? How much time will it take to serve on the session? Some of these questions may have been answered by the nominating committee; others will be answered during the time of preparation. But you consented to serve if elected because you love your church and wish to do your part in serving it.

This book is intended to provide some answers to your questions about eldership in the Presbyterian Church: the duties of elders and how to perform them more effectively. With other materials you will be examining, it will help you to find satisfaction in your service to the church. You will not find all you may wish to know in these pages. There is much more to learn, and there is a wealth of resources to help you.

The Presbyterian Church from its beginnings has placed great emphasis on the leadership of laypersons, both as reflecting the will of God for the church and as essential for the vitality of the church. Consequently your training, at this period and throughout your service as an elder, is of prime importance. Among the most interesting aspects of your work to which you may look forward is the opportunity for self-improvement and growth in which you will be engaged with your pastor and fellow officers.

Yours is an essential and important task. The Presbyterian Church holds it in honor. May you find increasing joy in the performance of your duties as a faithful servant of Jesus Christ.

Quotations from the Form of Government (e.g., G-10.0101) are from *The Constitution of the Presbyterian Church (U.S.A.),* Part II: *Book of Order,* 1985–86.

I
God Calls Persons to Serve

You are a Protestant and you belong to a particular branch of Protestantism called "Reformed." Even more particularly, you are a member of the Presbyterian Church in that family of Reformed churches. This particularity makes a big difference when you, as a layperson, seek to define your relationship to the church. You may have taken it quite for granted that as a church member you are called upon to teach in the education program, to serve on committees that determine the program of your church, to assist the pastor in parish visitation, or to perform the many other tasks necessary to the ministry and mission of your congregation. You may have participated in worship as a liturgist, preacher, or member of the choir. Whatever part you may have taken in the life of your church, you have correctly assumed, because you are a Christian and a church member, that you have the right and duty to be more than a spectator or a passive recipient of work done by "professionals." In a very real sense, laypersons *are* the church.

Let us take this thought a little further. Is the distinction we commonly make between laypersons and clergy a valid one? Certainly in such fields of human endeavor as medicine or law it is valid to differentiate between laypersons and professionals. Doctors and lawyers have specialized knowledge and skills that the rest of us do not possess, and we would be foolish not to recognize and avail ourselves of their competencies. But is this true also in matters of religion?

There are hierarchical churches that teach that this distinction must be recognized within church order. They hold that two orders of believers were created by Christ, a clerical order, with a unique status in relation to God, and a lay order, which stands in an inferior and different position ecclesiastically and functionally in the church. According to this concept there are gradations of spiritual authority, conferred by the rite of ordination into the succession of the apostles, in order that the church might be infallibly guided in all that pertains to right doctrine and moral living. All this is seen as a divine provision for the proper government of the church and for the nurture of the flock of God.

It is obvious that this is not the concept or practice of the Protestant church, and in particular it is not the way of the Presbyterian Church. The Form of Government of the Presbyterian Church (U.S.A.) states, "The church offices mentioned in the New Testament which this church has maintained include those of presbyters (ministers of the Word and elders) and deacons" (G-6.0103). It may sometimes appear that there are two classes of people in the church—ministers and laypersons—but our Constitution makes it clear that ministry, the work of the church, is one ministry. The difference between "lay" and "clergy" lies in particular functions performed by those who are ordained. "The existence of these offices [ministers of the Word, elders, and deacons] in no way diminishes the importance of the commitment of all members to the total ministry of the church" (G-6.0102).

Ministers of the Word are required to fulfill certain academic requirements; four years of college and three years of theological study are usually expected. They are then ordained by presbytery and perform certain functions which other persons do not, in particular the administration of the sacraments and moderating the session. If there is a valid distinction between "lay" and "clergy," it is at this point.

For Presbyterian Protestants, the following two things are clear regarding the relationship of clergy and laypersons.

1. *Priesthood is an office of every member of the church.* Each believer is a priest. "Members and officers alike serve mutually under the mandate of Christ who is the chief minister of all" (G-6.0101). We may all come to God without benefit of an intermediary because Christ is our Mediator. We may make our confessions and receive forgiveness by that right which our Lord has bestowed upon us. At the same time, all believers are to serve a priestly function to each other. In his pastoral letter, James exhorts believers to "confess your sins to one another, and pray for one another, that you may be healed" (James 5:16). Each person who is a forgiven sinner may be the channel of God's grace to another sinner who is seeking God's forgiveness and peace. Indeed, this loving service may be more effectively performed by a spiritually experienced Christian who is a friend than by an ordained minister. A part of our calling to be Christian bestows this privilege upon us.

The priesthood of all believers underlies the worship of a Protestant church. Worship is a corporate act in which all participate and in which each participant helps the other. This is particularly evident at the Lord's Table, where the presiding minister of the Word points to Jesus Christ as the host. With the people, the minister gives thanks for the gifts of bread and wine and sets them apart for their sacred use. The elements are passed from minister to officer and from person to person as dramatic evidence of the truth that we have one Redeemer and that we are all brothers and sisters. As persons partake of the bread and wine, they are led by the Holy Spirit to discern the Real within the symbol, to offer their own and others' needs to God, and to receive enabling grace. The emphasis is upon the conversation between each soul and Christ, who is really present by faith. Thus each acts as his or her own priest, in partaking, and as priest to others in passing the elements and in prayer for others.

The priesthood of all believers is most obvious in worship in the Sacrament of the Lord's Supper, but it exists in other parts of worship as well. Martin Luther observed that congregational singing is a priestly service in which each worshiper helps others to praise God. Greeting each other with an offering of God's peace and sharing mutual concerns and joys in prayer are means of grace within common worship. Leading our families in worship in the home and interceding with love for friends, neighbors, and those in need of God's grace are special ways in which every believer acts as priest. When we are what we ought to be, every believer in Christ is one through whom others may come to God and God's grace may be poured out upon them.

2. *This relationship between persons in the Presbyterian Church is also seen in our concept of ordination.* By ordination we refer to a religious rite practiced certainly from very early times in the Christian church (Acts 6:6; 13:3; 1 Tim. 4:14; 5:22). It is based upon the conviction that the Holy Spirit bestows gifts on believers for the common good (1 Cor. 12:4–11). We acknowledge these gifts of special tasks and skills by ordaining, or "setting apart" through the laying on of hands, certain persons to offices in the church. Thus distinctions which may be made in the Presbyterian system are based on functions and on the recognition of those special gifts bestowed

by the Holy Spirit that are to be used for the good of all.

Ministers of the Word are to "be responsible for a quality of life and relationships that commend the gospel to all persons and that communicate its joy and its justice. The pastor is responsible for studying, teaching, and preaching the Word, for administering Baptism and the Lord's Supper, for praying with and for the congregation" (G-6.0202). Most of these duties are to be shared with others, specifically with elders and deacons, and this section of the *Book of Order* goes on to indicate how this is to be done (G-6.0202, continued).

> Elders are chosen by the people. Together with ministers of the Word, they exercise leadership, government, and discipline and have responsibilities for the life of a particular church as well as the church-at-large, including ecumenical relationships. . . . It is the duty of elders, individually and jointly, to strengthen and nurture the faith and life of the congregation committed to their charge. . . . Those duties which all Christians are bound to perform by the law of love are especially incumbent upon elders because of their calling to office and are to be fulfilled by them as official responsibilities. (G-6.0300, 0304)

> The office of deacon as set forth in Scripture is one of sympathy, witness, and service after the example of Jesus Christ. . . . It is the duty of deacons, first of all, to minister to those who are in need, to the sick, to the friendless, and to any who may be in distress. (G-6.0400)

Since we are concerned in this book with the work of the elder, let us look for a moment at some points of similarity and difference between the office of elder and that of minister of the Word. As presbyters (those having governance and serving as members of governing bodies in the church), elders and ministers of the Word have equal standing. The vote of elders in sessions, presbyteries, synods, and General Assemblies counts just as much as does that of ministers of the Word. General Assembly is made up of equal numbers of elders and ministers of the Word, and in presbyteries and synods the numbers are approximately equal. Obviously, there is little if any distinction made between the two offices in the governance of the church. On the contrary, there is significant parity between them. This is important in the life of the Presbyterian Church.

But there are differences. Elders do not labor in "word and doctrine." This is required of ministers of the Word and, if it is to be done in a fitting and profitable manner, requires special training and faithful preparation (2 Tim. 2:15). Ministers of the Word will, therefore, ordinarily be more skilled in preaching and teaching the Word. Indeed, such persons may be said to have been called by the Holy Spirit to this vocation, for which academic discipline is intended to make them worthy workers. So by divine call and by training, the minister of the Word occupies a position of unique value and responsibility in relation to the flock of Christ. Ministers of the Word are honored and respected not because of any attributes or powers within themselves, but because of the calling of God and the training they have received for their work.

Our Reformed heritage causes us to take a dim view of "professionalism" and "specialists" in matters of faith. Faith is an encounter with God. The truth of the Christian faith is not some secret learning to which only certain initiates have access; neither is it a spiritual power which only some possess and can transmit. The heart of our faith is that Christ comes to persons whom the Spirit has awakened to faith. It is a perversion to think of our faith in terms of "professionalism." We would not tolerate professionals responsible for praying for us any more than we would tolerate professionals responsible for showing

Christian love. The church is true to itself and its Lord when there are *not* two classes of people—one with a unique status in relation to the things of God and another standing in an inferior position.

Now let us look briefly at the history of the Christian church so that we may be reminded how, from its beginning, laypersons have been inherently a part of its order and life.

The New Testament provides ample evidence that God calls laypersons to labor in and through the church. Immediately we think of those whom Jesus chose to be with him, none of them members of the religious establishment. Peter was a fisherman; Matthew a tax gatherer. Except for Nicodemus, no rulers of the synagogue or of the temple hierarchy are mentioned among those close to Jesus. It is significant that he chose lay women and men who had a capacity for growth and loyalty and who were willing to give themselves courageously to a spiritual mission. This is another example of how God bypasses the establishment in order to get on with God's purpose in the world.

The same evidence is found in the Old Testament. With few exceptions, the prophets and other leaders were laypersons, chosen by God for the often difficult and dangerous task of calling the people back to the path God had chosen for them. There is an openness of heart to the Spirit of the living God that is characteristic of those whom God chooses for places of leadership and responsibility.

After the death and resurrection of Christ, there was little sign of formal organization among his followers. Peter seems to have been their accepted spokesperson, but as he began his missionary journeys it was James, Jesus' brother, who assumed leadership in the Christian community in Jerusalem. In the beginning, the company of believers continued to live and worship very much as they had before

Jesus came. They worshiped in the Temple and doubtless attended the synagogues. But as their numbers grew and they were scattered throughout Palestine and abroad, they were more and more excluded from the synagogue fellowship. As the Christians grew more conscious of their new identity in Christ, they found themselves becoming separate from Judaism. The strong leadership of Paul and the rapid spread of Christianity among the Gentiles hastened this process. Consequently, the small communities of Christians throughout the cities and towns of the Roman Empire began to organize themselves, usually around the pattern of the synagogue with which they were familiar.

The synagogue was a democratic institution that had come into being at the time of the destruction of the Temple and the captivity of Israel in Babylon. It came to have such importance to the Jews scattered in communities around the Roman Empire that, even after the restoration of Temple worship in Jerusalem, these synagogues continued to have a major role in fostering religious life. Mention is frequently made in the New Testament of the "elders of the synagogue." These were probably older men whose prestige among the people elevated them to positions of oversight and trust. Leadership was often a function of age and experience; even in the Roman senate and elsewhere, the rulers of the people, judges and magistrates, were selected from among the elderly. In time the title "elder" was applied to certain leaders regardless of the age of the person.

When, as we have said, Christians became separated from the Jewish community and began to form communities of their own, they patterned both their worship and their organization after that of the synagogue. Thus, just as there had been elders in the synagogue who were entrusted with rule and order as well as the teaching of the people, so in the early Christian communities elders were appointed by the founders of the churches or chosen by the people themselves. The responsibilities of these persons were particularly heavy, because the original apostles became fewer in number with the passing of the years, and they devoted most of their time to missionary work. Those who were trained and appointed by the apostles as preachers and teachers also traveled from place to place, founding new congregations and making converts. When these persons were not present, the nurture and discipline of the congregation fell upon the shoulders of the elders. Naturally they came to be persons who were highly esteemed and invaluable to the church. The measure of respect and confidence in which they were held by the apostle Paul is evident in the touching story in Acts 20:17–38, where he summons the elders of the church in Ephesus to Miletus for a conference and a parting word of encouragement and farewell. It is impossible to measure how much of the spread and the continuing strength of the early church was due to the efforts of these early elders. It was they who preserved in large part the integrity of the faith and who in times of persecution rallied the flock to stand firm.

In the centuries that followed, this democratic lay-administered organization of the church gradually weakened. As the church grew in numbers and importance, there developed a hierarchical structure in which the administration of the church and its work of preaching, teaching, and worship were placed more and more in the hands of the clergy. The consequence was that laity were excluded from all responsible participation in and direction of religious activities. The lay movement did not die out, however. Certain lay orders arose within the church and fostered a life of piety and good deeds. These communities of humble faith and service kept alive a genuine spiritual glow during centuries we sometimes call the Dark

Ages. To them also we owe the preservation of the Scriptures and much of the art, music, liturgy, and sense of mission and ministry that belong to Christ's church.

At the beginning of the sixteenth century, the time was ripe for change and renewal. With reforms in politics, economics, and learning came a corresponding religious movement known as the Reformation. The purpose of its leaders was not to start a new church but to cleanse the existing institution of abuses and impurities. It was sparked by a rediscovery of the faith of the early Christians to which the New Testament bore witness. For our purposes we shall confine our story to the Reformation in Geneva, Switzerland, of which John Calvin was the leader. The beginnings of the Presbyterian system of doctrine and church government lie there.

For his organizational model, Calvin used the church of the second century. We have mentioned that there is little in the New Testament or in other historical material about the organization of the very early church. Indeed, there seems to have been little in the way of formal organization among the early companies of Christians. They held that the Holy Spirit distributed gifts among the faithful to be used to benefit the whole group (1 Cor. 12:4–11), and the whole congregation assumed responsibility for its own order and discipline as its circumstances and location demanded. A better-articulated system developed during the second century. Calvin held that Christ had instituted in the church the four offices of pastor, teacher, ruling elder, and deacon. Pastors were to preach the Word of God, teachers were to establish schools for the education of the young and the instruction of adults (the beginning of the public school system and the Presbyterian emphasis upon Christian education), ruling elders were to maintain order and discipline, and deacons were to administer charities for the relief of the poor and destitute.

In Calvin's Geneva, the ruling elders were laymen, twelve in number, who represented the various parishes in the city and related both to the church and to the civil government. They took an oath similar to that prescribed for ministers. They met once each week with the pastors in a body known as the consistory to hear complaints against immoralities, indecent language, doctrinal error, or other matters that might corrupt the purity of the church and bring reproach upon its good name. At the end of the year the elders presented themselves to the magistrates, who decided whether they had faithfully performed their duties and should be kept in office.

Here we have the elements characteristic of Presbyterian ecclesiastical life and discipline. Here were ministers and laymen with equal authority, but who with a division of responsibility and labor served the church for its edification and order. The system was somewhat modified when this family of the Reformation spread beyond Geneva. Civil authority became much less closely tied to the church, and ruling elders came to be elected by members of the congregation and not appointed by the councils of municipal government. Yet they continued to be entrusted with the "peace, unity, and purity" of the church, and so, to distinguish their office from that of pastors, they were called "ruling elders."

From Geneva, Calvin's Reformation spread to Scotland, to north Ireland, to Holland, and from the old world to the new. During this migration it never lost the essentials of its ecclesiastical structure. In any Presbyterian church, regardless of size or location, the session is the superior authority charged with responsibility for the whole life of the congregation. Ministers and elders—both ordained—under the guidance of the Holy Spirit, work together to present every person "mature in Christ" (Col. 1:28).

II
Who Qualifies
for Eldership?

Sue was proud and happy that her church had just elected her as an elder. It was gratifying that this confidence had been placed in her. She had grown up in the church, taught in the church school, and served on the youth council of the presbytery. She had expressed some doubts when the nominating committee visited with an invitation to allow her name to be placed on the ballot. After the committee members left, she had called her father, who was also an elder. He was delighted at her news. "Your question is the same as mine when I was first asked," he told her. "Am I good enough to be an elder?"

At the time Sue was twenty-two years old. Perhaps her youth had something to do with her doubts. As we noted in the first chapter, from earliest times in every society, the old men have been asked to give counsel and leadership to the people; hence the term "elder." Sue was not sure she had had sufficient experience for the wisdom she would need to be an elder and give spiritual leadership to others.

But in the matter of age, society—and the church with it—has changed considerably in its viewpoint. The performance and insights of young people who are open to the leading of the Holy Spirit, and who wish to serve others, are impressive and convincing. Both the Constitution of the church and its practice urge that they contribute their talents as officers. Years have relatively little to do with being "good enough" to be an elder. Right qualifications are not paced by the calendar. The church has found that it is greatly to its advantage to avail itself of the gifts and services of its younger members.

It has been only in comparatively recent years that the church has permitted women to serve as elders. Even more recently, women have been ordained as ministers of the Word. The wisdom of these actions has already been amply demonstrated in the effective leadership that women have given to the church as elders and ministers. We are realizing the truth of the apostle Paul's statement that in Christ "there is neither male nor female; for you are all one in Christ Jesus" (Gal. 3:28).

Of more immediate pertinence, however, are two other considerations: What must an elder *believe,* and what must an elder *be?* In this chapter we shall consider the first.

What must an elder believe? The Constitution of the church requires, at the time of ordination of elders, that nine questions be put to the candidates to which affirmative answers are required. The first three questions deal with one's personal religious faith, the last six with the duties of the elder (Form of Government, ch. XIV, sec. 2). A careful reading of the questions dealing with personal faith serve to indicate what an elder must believe.

The first question is about Jesus Christ: "Do you trust in Jesus Christ your Savior, acknowledge him Lord of all and Head of the church, and through him believe in one God, Father, Son, and Holy Spirit?" (G-14.0207a).

Central to the identity of all Christians is faith in Jesus

Christ. The earliest of the creeds was probably the simple statement, Jesus is Lord. Thus those who are set apart by ordination are required to affirm their commitment to Christ. He is the one who, born in human flesh, shared our life fully. He is the one we confess to be the true and complete revelation of God. In Christ we discover the meaning and purpose of all that God intends for human life.

Presbyterians, along with all other Christians, are monotheists and trinitarians. By monotheists we mean that we conceive of God as one and not many. God, as Father, Son, and Holy Spirit, is not three gods but one God. Yet Christians differ from other monotheists (Jews and Muslims) in their idea of the nature of the unity that is God. The idea that the "three are one" may sound like an impossible dilemma to some, and because it is hard and superficially illogical there have been those, like the Unitarians, who have been willing to abandon the doctrine of the Trinity. But throughout the history of the church there has been a stubborn insistence that within the unity of God there is a rich, if unfathomable, differentiation which we name "Father, Son, and Holy Spirit."

This doctrine is not the invention of theologians; indeed, it is not an invention at all. It was formulated out of the experience of those who, through the ages, were confronted by the living God. The overpowering religious experience came first, followed by the effort to define the experience in terms of doctrine. There are depths in the nature of God which finite creatures will never fully know, for God is infinite. Yet the revelation of God that we know through God's dealings with humankind is authentic and many-sided. These are the data on which our understanding of God rests. In trying to interpret them, we arrive at the doctrine of the Trinity. The clue to understanding the doctrine is the question, "How has God actually been revealed in human experience?" The Bible provides source material for an answer.

The writer of the book of Hebrews declared that "in many and various ways God spoke of old to our ancestors by the prophets" (Heb. 1:1). God did not speak in audible words but in mighty deeds. The revelation that God gave was not only information about God's own nature but also the way in which God's living presence was perceived in acts by those whose hearts had been opened by the Spirit of God (Eph. 1:18). To such enlightened persons the creation spoke of the "glory of God" and the firmament showed God's "handiwork" (Ps. 19:1). God's purpose was read in certain acts in history, notably in the redemption of Israel from bondage in Egypt and the experiences incident to the settling of Canaan. We have no universally convincing explanation why the prophets of Israel discerned in the events of their history the hand of God, but they each attributed to those events the work of the supreme Sovereign, one who was all holy, all wise, and all just. We do not know how they came to believe that the destiny of the world and of their own people in particular was to be found in God's will to rule in righteousness and mercy. What is clear from the Bible is that this idea was firmly fixed in their view of things and that it explained for them the meaning both of past events and of the future yet to be. Faith in the one true God inspired confidence in the covenant God had made with their people and the expectation that God would bless them as they sought to be a blessing to all people.

The same writer of Hebrews then goes on to say, "But in these last days God has spoken to us by a Son, whom God appointed the heir of all things, through whom also God created the world" (Heb. 1:2). The writers of the New Testament were convinced that in telling the story of

Jesus they were proclaiming the greatest of the mighty events in history, in which the eternal purpose of God to visit and redeem God's people had transpired (Luke 1:68). They called their proclamation the "gospel" because it was the good news that in Jesus Christ the living God was present in their midst, bringing forgiveness of sins and salvation in new life. They did not write about Jesus as though he were another messenger who brought new tidings about God, although this is certainly a part of what he did; but they declared that, in the person, the life, the death, the resurrection, and the ascension into glory of Jesus, God had achieved salvation, bringing reconciliation and triumph over sin and death. Jesus was God's deed!

Writer after writer, preacher after preacher in the New Testament, found the experience of Jesus so overwhelming that language was too poor a vehicle to express the joy and adoration awakened by it (Eph. 1:3; 1 Peter 1:3–4; 1 John 4:9). Each reveals a spirit of joy and triumph that pervades the New Testament. But even more, each writer points to the source of that joy and confidence as the salvation event that is inseparably united with the person and work of Christ. They were so possessed by the wonder of what God had done in Christ, and so engrossed in proclaiming the good news, that they had no time to theologize about it; that task was left to later generations. But a new dimension within the being of God had been opened to them in the person of Jesus, and henceforth in their minds and hearts Jesus Christ and God were one within the bounds of a uniquely divine relationship.

The words in which they reported their experience and declared their faith might lead us to surmise that after his resurrection and ascension Jesus was no longer among them. They preached that he was in heaven "seated at the right hand of God." Jesus was given the "name which is above every name" and was to be called "Lord" (Phil. 2:9–11). Yet it is important to remember that even as they ascribed honor and power to him, they did not conceive of him as absent from them. On the contrary, their deepest conviction was that "I am with you always, to the close of the age" (Matt. 28:20).

The real but unseen presence of Christ among his follow- ers was attributed by them to the sending of the Spirit. The Spirit did not take the place of Christ but enabled his followers to realize that Christ had never left them. The Lord continued to be among his disciples in the reality of his spiritual presence, through which he continued to teach them and to empower them for effective witness and right living. They believed that the Holy Spirit had been the means by which the prophets had discerned God in the events of history. The language of writers in both the New and Old Testaments leads us to assume that they did not differentiate between their experience of God realized as actively present and the influence of the Holy Spirit. Yet the Spirit is not confused with God or with Christ, from whom the Spirit is sent.

Here then is a threefold experience of the divine which is one. We can make no sense of the doctrine of the Trin- ity unless we too have experienced God's reconciling the world to God in Christ and effecting reconciliation in our hearts through God's Spirit. The logic of the doctrine is in religious experience. We may try to penetrate the mystery of the "three in one," but we are better off simply to affirm that though we cannot know the depths of the being of God, we can experience God's justice, God's salvation, and God's living presence.

The second question concerns the Scriptures: "Do you accept the Scriptures of the Old and New Testaments to be, by the Holy Spirit, the unique and authoritative witness to Jesus Christ in the church universal, and God's Word to you?" (G-14.0207b).

What does it mean to accept the Scriptures of the Old and New Testaments as God's Word to you? This involves us in the consideration of what we mean by the "Word of God." Certainly we do not mean literally a written document or an audible message directly from God to a human being. When we read, "The word of the Lord came to the prophet saying . . ." there is no description as to how the word was received. It is sometimes declared to have come through dreams or visions, which in earlier times were thought to be the media through which God communicated to humanity. Usually, however, the word of God came in connection with some important crisis in the life of the individual or the nation. As we reflect upon the experiences of God's people as told in the Bible, we may infer that the "Word" was God personally present and active in a situation whose meaning was discerned by the prophet, who was also involved by the work of the Spirit. Thus God "spoke" both in the event and in the divine significance discerned by the prophet. What was "seen" or "heard" was preached as the Word of the Lord. In words, the prophets declared the Word. When these were finally written they became a part of the Bible.

The ordination question refers to the Word as being the unique and authoritative witness to Jesus Christ. For all Christians, Jesus Christ is the living Word of God. In him the creative Word by which God made the universe, the eternal Reality which is the source of mind and freedom in humankind, was personally present. The Word of God is Person. All that the New Testament says about Christ, it says about the Word. Thus the question asks us to differentiate between the Word of God and words about the Word which are found in the Bible and which witness to the living Word.

A further observation must be made, however. Except for the Old Testament we have no record of the way in which God communicated God's purposes and will for the redemption of humankind through specific acts related to the people whom God called and with whom God covenanted. Nor have we, except for the New Testament, any record of the continuation and climactic fulfillment in Jesus Christ of this same redemptive work of God. The relation between the Word of God and the Scriptures is not accidental. The living Word awakened and inspired the writers of the Bible and ever since has illuminated the hearts and incited response in those who read it. We read the Scripture in order to discern in its words the very Word of God—God's Word to us.

Truth is the supreme authority in faith and practice. We Presbyterian Protestants find that truth in the living Word to which the Scriptures testify. The living Word who is God, known to us in Jesus Christ through the Holy Spirit, stands above every other authority. By this Word the church is judged, recognizes its need for reforming, seeks God's peace, reforms both itself and other human institutions, stands with all who are oppressed, and looks always to its Savior and Head as it seeks to embody Christ in God's world.

The third question reads: "Do you sincerely receive and adopt the essential tenets of the Reformed faith as expressed in the confessions of our church as authentic and reliable expositions of what Scripture leads us to believe and do, and will you be instructed and led by those confessions as you lead the people of God?" (G-14.0207c).

The Presbyterian Church is a confessional church. Through the years, Christians in various places and circumstances have said strongly what they believe about God, about the church, about humankind, and about the activity of God and God's people in the world which is God's. Thus our confessions are important, particularly to those of us who have been called to serve as leaders.

The Form of Government indicates the importance of the confessions when it states, "In these confessional statements the church declares to its members and to the world who and what it is, what it believes, and what it resolves to do. These statements identify the church as a community of people known by its convictions as well as by its actions" (G-2.0100).

The *Book of Confessions* is a collection of statements of faith in the form of declarations, catechisms, creeds, and confessions made by the church throughout history. Each was formed in a time when the church faced a crisis and found it necessary to declare what it believed. The church reformed its life and mission as required by the will of God, revealed by the Holy Spirit through the living Word. These confessional statements unite us with those who have gone before us, and whose collective experience of the living God guides our own understanding of who we are, what we believe, and what we will do in God's name. Thus the confessions are more than historical documents. "They guide the church in its study and interpretation of the Scriptures; they summarize the essence of Christian tradition; they direct the church in maintaining sound doctrines; they equip the church for its work in proclamation" (G-2.0100). In receiving these confessions we admit their value and accept their guidance. In adopting them, we attempt to make them our own and form our faith and ministry from them in our own day.

It is important to note that these are referred to as "essential tenets" of the Reformed faith. This means that we are not required to receive and adopt everything the confessions say. Remembering that they each reflect a particular time and a particular necessity, we acknowledge that they may at times vary from our current convictions. For example, the Scots Confession condemns the "error of the Anabaptists, who deny that children should be baptized before they have faith and understanding" (*Book of Confessions,* 3.23). And certain passages of the Westminster Confession of Faith (ch. X), felt to contain inferences that called for a more explicit statement of faith, were clarified by the church in 1903. Because the church is always being reformed by the Word of God, the confessions cannot be taken as a literal and complete statement of our present faith. These texts are not a straitjacket, binding our minds, but flags around which we may rally or anchors to steady the church against being "carried about with every wind of doctrine" (Eph. 4:14). When the church knows what it believes and can declare it clearly, it is in the strongest possible position to fulfill its Christian task.

A common theological thread runs through all the confessions despite differences in language, time of writing, and issues addressed. There are five major themes in Reformed doctrine that are identified in the Form of Government (G-2.0500) and that may be considered "essential tenets."

1. "The majesty, holiness, and providence of God." God is above all, through all, and in all. Nothing is beyond the concern and the love of God.

2. "The election of the people of God for service as well as for salvation." We are called as a people by God, and to respond in faith is to serve God and do God's will in the whole earth.

3. "Covenant life marked by a disciplined concern for order in the church according to the Word of God." We are a community of people bound together by God to keep the church faithful from age to age. This task informs the nature of our life together.

4. "A faithful stewardship that shuns ostentation and seeks proper use of the gifts of God's creation." The world is a part of God's good creation, and the faithful are stewards of this household *(oikumenē)*. As such we are responsible to God to live simply and in harmony with one another and the world.

5. "The recognition of the human tendency to idolatry and tyranny." Sin is both personal and corporate. As obedient servants of a loving and forgiving God, we stand against all oppression and injustice, as does God. We all stand as equals before God, a fact that informs our ordination, for we are "set apart" to serve with others and not over them.

The third ordination question is an important supplement to the first two. We fulfill our office through obedience to Jesus Christ; this is first and central. We do so under the authority of the Scriptures, which bear witness to the Lordship of Christ. We are guided by the confessions as reliable expositions of Scripture. Our confessions lead and instruct us as we seek to be faithful servants of God through Jesus Christ and under the power of the Holy Spirit.

III
What Must
an Elder Be?

Faith and character are intimately related. What we believe is reflected in our lives, and, conversely, what we do has determinative influence on our faith. Our lives speak far more convincingly than our words. The Form of Government states, "Elders should be persons of faith, dedication, and good judgment. Their manner of life should be a demonstration of the Christian gospel, both within the church and in the world" (G-6.0303). It is important that elders be worthy people, but how do we gauge fitness of character?

If we look at those Jesus chose to be with him, we probably would not pick many of them as elders! There was Peter, emotionally volcanic, unpredictable, capable of great loyalty and courage yet who cringed before a servant and violently denied his discipleship, slow to acknowledge the faith of Gentiles, and vacillating in his convictions regarding the freedom and privileges of his new faith. There was Matthew, a tax gatherer, whose odious profession had dishonored him among his own people. Judas had a fatal flaw that was not apparent on the surface of his life. Neither these nor the other disciples were perfect persons, yet they were the ones Jesus chose, and what was accomplished through them is a marvel and a miracle.

Reflect for a moment on what Jesus accomplished through Peter. Matthew's Gospel records Jesus as saying to Peter, "You are Peter, and on this rock I will build my church" (Matt. 16:18). Can a more important role be imagined? The incidents that transpired in the Christian community immediately after the death and resurrection of Jesus, as related in the early chapters of Acts, show a strong and stable Peter as guide, counselor, and spokesperson for the whole group. Peter was the central figure in the early church at Jerusalem, wisely guiding the infant church through times of crisis, internal friction, and external danger. He did, indeed, become a rock in a crucial time when a less courageous and committed disciple would have failed to meet the need of the hour.

This observation should serve to encourage a person who is asked to be an elder to accept the office and not be too concerned about being "worthy." It is perhaps inevitable that anyone called by God to exercise leadership in the church should hesitate to respond at once to the summons. The spiritual demands of the task make anyone feel inadequate. This is characteristic even of persons in the Bible. When God summoned Moses from the burning bush to deliver the people from the hand of Pharaoh, his response was, "Who am I that I should go to Pharaoh, and bring the sons of Israel out of Egypt?" (Ex. 3:11). In the temple, Isaiah had a vision from which he recoiled because the revealing light had exposed his soul: "I am a man of unclean lips . . . for my eyes have seen the King, the LORD of hosts!" (Isa. 6:5). Jeremiah lamented his youth and weakness when called by God to be a messenger. But in each case, God gave assurance that grace would be sufficient to make them useful servants of God—and all of them performed conspicuous service.

So if our immediate reaction to the invitation to be an

elder is "I'm not the person for the job; there must be others better fitted for it," we are following a familiar pattern. But the matter should not end there, for that is where the conversation really begins! What personal qualifications fit one for the duties of this office? "Am I 'spiritual' enough?" "I'm the trustee type; I feel at home in the business world and am confident in the sort of decision-making that requires. But I'm uncertain about being an elder." "I believe in the church, but I'm not a person who prays a lot. Doesn't an elder have to do that?"

Perhaps we can arrive at a clearer understanding of what an elder must be if we approach the question under two heads: the elder's qualifications as a Christian and a church member and the elder's special qualifications as an officer in the church.

Qualifications as a Christian and a Church Member

The sixth ordination question asks, "Will you in your own life seek to follow the Lord Jesus Christ, love your neighbors, and work for the reconciliation of the world?" (G-14.0207f). It is assumed that the elder will be a Christian. It is difficult to define precisely what makes a person a Christian—we may be arbitrarily too sharp or too vague in drawing the picture—but let us make an attempt.

A Christian is a "committed" person. The life of the Christian belongs to Jesus Christ. The Christian has heard the message of God's love revealed in Jesus Christ and has realized that this love lays claim to his or her own life. The apostle Paul expressed it this way: "I appeal to you therefore, brethren, by the mercies of God, to present your bodies as a living sacrifice, holy and acceptable to God, which is your spiritual worship. Do not be conformed to this world but be transformed by the renewal of your mind, that you may prove what is the will of God, what is good and acceptable and perfect" (Rom. 12:1–2). A two-fold response is involved in this appeal, both a firm initial decision—"present your bodies as a living sacrifice"—and a consequent development of the spiritual life—"be transformed by the renewal of your mind." These two are joined to each other. We cannot present our bodies as a living sacrifice without going on to a daily surrender of our minds and hearts to the Spirit of God, by which we come to see and feel and act from a point of view very different from that which characterizes the world that is not under the rule of Christ. We need to remember here that Paul implied more than the physical body. He refers to one's personality at its fullest and most effective embodiment and expression; it is the whole person who is dedicated to Christ.

We may change the metaphor from sacrifice to citizenship. When we understand our status as Christians, we shall know that we have changed our citizenship; our subjection is no longer to the world of false ideals, wrong objectives, and unworthy motives by which we were once influenced. Our loyalty is now to Christ and Christ's rule in everything. It is this decision to let the will of God as revealed in Jesus Christ determine every aspect of life that makes a person a Christian. It calls for worship and obedience; it results in the transformation of character, whereby we are less and less imitators of the world and the "worldly" and more and more living expressions of God's Spirit.

As we reflect on all this, it becomes obvious that an elder is more than a good person, a rigorously ethical or even a kind and generous person. An elder is a Christian, and there is a difference. The difference is in one's faithfulness to God. There are many who are model citizens, honest in business, cordial in relationships, community-minded, and advocates of right living. But essential to being a Christian is the awareness that a conversation is constantly taking place between the person and God, and that the person's part in the conversation leads to worship, repentance, commitment, and new life. A Christian may or may not be morally better than others, but whatever the Christian does will be done in the awareness that it is done in the sight of God. When the Christian does wrong, he or she recognizes that this is more than breaking a law, it is, in the words of the psalmist, "Against thee, thee only, have I sinned, and done that which is evil in thy sight" (Ps. 51:4). For the Christian, sin is a personal breach of loyalty.

By the same token, "righteousness" is not just correct character, but grateful trust in God who loves us, and an acceptance of God's will for our lives. Character inevitably grows out of our faith, but it is not a substitute for faith. So elders will wish to grow in their experience of God. Worship, both private and corporate, will be a valued practice. Reading and studying the Scripture will be a part of their discipline. Their lives will be constantly seeking to give the Spirit control over all their words and deeds.

There may be moments when elders, like all persons, feel despair in their attempts to achieve praiseworthy spiritual lives, even as Paul confessed that he had not attained (Phil. 3:12). But elders will be useful to God nevertheless, if they persist as did the apostle when he wrote, "Forgetting what lies behind and straining forward to what lies ahead, I press on toward the goal for the prize of the upward call of God in Christ Jesus" (Phil. 3:13–14).

Qualifications as a Church Officer

One would hope that what has just been said would constitute sufficient qualifications for election to the elder-

ship. Those who were chosen as leaders of the early
church were described as persons "of good repute, full of
the Spirit and of wisdom" (Acts 6:3), which implies that
they were esteemed by the community, deeply and sincerely religious in spirit, and practical in judgment. Yet
there is something more required of an elder. This quality
is hard to define and may be said to be included in what
we refer to as "leadership."

An elder is a member of a team. Ordination question
eight asks, "Will you seek to serve the people with energy,
intelligence, imagination, and love?" (G-14.0207h). The
elder must be cooperative and flexible. Firm convictions
and strong initiative are desirable qualities if they do not
lead to self-assertion or unbending insistence upon one's
own opinions. The Holy Spirit exercises leadership for the
fullest advantage to the church when working through
committed individuals as members of a group. Our church
government is based upon a Spirit-filled community which
chooses competent persons to represent them in the
spiritual ordering of the life of the church. "It is the duty
of elders, individually and jointly, to strengthen and nurture the faith and life of the congregation committed to
their charge" (G-6.0304). When the elders meet as a session they meet as Spirit-filled persons where private judg-
ments will be either confirmed by the consent of the rest
or corrected in the light which falls from other minds. This
does not mean that the group is always right and the
individual always wrong; but the government and discipline of the Presbyterian Church is firmly based upon the
conviction that the Spirit of God speaks to and through the
whole church, and not to special persons ecclesiastically
qualified. This principle also pervades a session meeting,
and however right an elder may think he or she is, if his

or her individuality disrupts the group spirit, the office of elder is not helpfully fulfilled. To be able to think with others, pray with others, and work with others is one of the qualifications of the elder.

In this relation, the seventh ordination question needs careful consideration: "Do you promise to further the peace, unity, and purity of the church?" (G-14.0207g). The elder is pledged to "study the peace . . . of the church." Peace is more than the absence of conflict. It is not a static condition in which affairs simply go on without change or variation. World peace is more than nations living quietly within set boundaries and disturbing each other as little as possible. It is never possible that this be true in a world of relentless change. Rather, peace is dynamic; it is purposeful and creative change. When we see leaders in politics, in business, and in related groups retooling economic policies and revamping national and international agreements and laws in the light of changing conditions and for the good of all the earth's people, that is a picture of world peace. The "peace of the church" is the church in creative action as it earnestly seeks to understand its mission and to fulfill it.

Thus the session is a body of believers open to change. Peace in the church is an alert congregation joyously and energetically fulfilling its mission as Christ's agent in the world. To study how this may happen is a concern of the elder.

Obviously there can be no peace where there is not unity. Paul pleads with the Christians at Philippi to complete his joy in Christ by "being of the same mind, having the same love, being in full accord and of one mind" (Phil. 2:2). He cites the example of Jesus as one who sought unity of spirit. As Jesus "emptied himself" of heavenly status and glory to take the form of a servant and even to die a shameful death upon a cross, so they must do nothing from conceit or selfishness, but be humble and look for the best interests of others (Phil. 2:3–4). No influence toward unity is more powerful in a church than this spirit demonstrated by the session. On the other hand, jealousy, hurt feelings, personal ambition, or party loyalties serve to mar the unity which the Holy Spirit would engender among elders and in the congregation. It is equally sad when division occurs between pastor and session. No quarrels are quite so damaging as religious quarrels because so much seems at stake. Yet this need not be true. Elders need not all hold the same opinion on matters of concerns to the church, but they must pray earnestly for forgiveness and reconciliation that the Holy Spirit may be sent into their hearts to bring peace and love. "To keep the unity of the Spirit in the bonds of peace" is incumbent upon every elder.

Lastly, the elder promises to study the "purity of the church." This implies that the church may be corrupted, and history bears out this sad truth. The elder will stand guard to see that the church is not corrupted in either its doctrine or its spirit, for from these come corruption in action.

The Presbyterian Church is a creedal church and regards right doctrine as of great importance. For the believer, the creeds and confessions are road maps; they help us find our way. They are not the way itself, any more than a road map is the road. But travelers need maps, and a faulty map is an unhappy deception. We are zealous for right teaching because we believe that the way of salvation through Jesus Christ can be described plainly enough that the seeker can find adequate help. But a caution must be inserted here: Just as a road map must from time to time be revised to bring it into line with the real and changing roads (we will not press the analogy any farther, as that would imply that the "way of salvation" changes), so theologies must be studied and restated to bring them into conformity with contemporary understanding of God's dealing with us for our well-being. Theologies are important, as are road maps, but they are the products of human thought about God's continuing self-revelation. So our attitude in defense of pure doctrine will be a reverent and humble teachableness in the revelation of God's will with a firm purpose to understand and define it as clearly as possible in the light of what has gone before and what is taking place at the present time. The Word of God speaking by the Spirit through the Scriptures is the standard for purity of doctrine. This message, as found in the creeds and confessions of the *Book of Confessions,* unites Presbyterians in their search for purity of doctrine.

The purity of the church must be defended in its life as in its doctrine. The church exists in and for God's world, a world that the Scriptures warn is both deceived and deceiver. Jesus refused to be enticed by the blandishments of the world and challenged his disciples to do likewise. That the church is "in but not of" the world is an important distinction. We are called to be holy as the Lord is holy.

This is not the place to discuss worldliness at length. In the memory of many, worldliness consisted of dancing, playing cards, attending the theater, profanity, failing to keep the Sabbath, and more. Purity in the church consisted of banning such evil practices. If this were brought up in session meeting today, there would doubtless be differences of opinion. But worldliness cannot be discussed helpfully until we realize that it is more subtle than a catalog of questionable practices might indicate. If it consisted only of overt "sins" we might be able, on our own, to combat it. Indeed, we do so, but it is just the unimpeachable lives of most church members that dull us to the real worldliness that blights us. For worldliness is the reign of the spirit of evil just as purity is the reign of the Spirit of Christ.

"The kingdom of evil," writes John Oman,

> is idolatry, so organized by hypocrisy that it is able to set itself up as the true order of the world. Valuing its neighbor only for itself, it makes possession the end and humankind the means, and turns the whole world into a temple for its idol, where it worships with all its mind and with all its heart and with all its strength. By the dazzling liturgy of all the worldly interests that appeal to selfish desire, it blinds its own eyes as well as the eyes of others, till its idol is accepted as the only true might in the world, over against which a rule of love seems mere fantasy and cloud-land. Nor did this idolatry ever erect a ritual so imposing as the material conquests of the present order of competition with its vast material equipment; nor was it ever so much taken at its face value as when thus enormously staged; nor has society ever been set by it on a more selfish foundation or been so robbed of the true uses of the world; nor has it ever issued in vaster destruction.
>
> (John Oman, *Grace and Reality,* p. 34; Cambridge University Press, 4th ed., 1931)

Professor Oman's characterization of the kingdom of evil bears pondering by elders. What are truly our concerns for the purity of the church? How much time and energy do we spend arguing about what constitute evil practices to the exclusion of the deeper concerns of greed, oppression, injustice, and warfare that are currently tearing apart the fabric of peace both in the church and in the world? How willing are we to "bear the cross" of being misunderstood or opposed or even vilified when we insist upon probing deep enough to begin to root out the underlying causes of the world's unrest and injustices that have their foundation in alienation from God's will for peace and shalom?

Those who call themselves disciples must dare to drink of the cup from which Christ drank and receive the baptism with which he was baptized. We must face boldly the challenges of worldliness, and not let ourselves in comfort live a worldly life under the illusion that we are still Christian. May God spare us the easy pleasure of having escaped the shattering judgment of Christ's cross by which alone the sham of this world's pretension is exposed. A great Danish philosopher once said, "Purity of heart is to will one thing." The psalmist cried, "One thing have I asked of the LORD, that will I seek after." Purity in the church comes through single-minded dedication to its Lord.

IV
The Session

"The session of a particular church consists of the pastor or co-pastors, the associate pastors, and the elders in active service" (G-10.0101).

"The session is responsible for the mission and government of the particular church" (G-10.0102). Chapter X of the Form of Government of the Presbyterian Church (U.S.A.) then lists eighteen specific duties and responsibilities of the session, ranging from the reception and dismissal of members to providing for their worship and nurture (including the nurture and spiritual growth of members of the session itself), to the continuing relationship with other governing bodies in the denomination and, beyond, to global and ecumenical relationships. Thus the duties of the session are many and varied. Responsibilities sometimes called administrative, in order to distinguish them from those thought of as spiritual, are linked by the Constitution in such a way as to enhance the spiritual dimension of all that the session does. Responsibility for budgets, property, maintenance, salaries, and program supervision are recognized as requiring gifts of the Holy Spirit just as the ministry of the ordained elder is understood to be a part of the whole ministry of the people of God.

One of the great satisfactions of serving on the session is the opportunity to establish lasting friendships with others of like dedication and purpose. Women and men who serve as elders find that this service affords them the chance to share in deep and significant ways with their peers on the session and to grow in the knowledge and love of God and their associates in ministry. Indeed, one of the duties of the session is "to engage in a process for education and mutual growth of the members of the session" (G-10.0102j).

The size of the session will differ with each congregation and is usually determined by the manner in which the congregation does its work and by the numerical strength of the membership. While the form of government is the same for all Presbyterian churches, the Constitution does not specify either the size of the session or its method of organization. These details are left to the discretion of each congregation and to the elders who have been chosen by it. The Form of Government does specify that "a quorum of the session shall be the pastor or other presiding officer and one third of the elders, except for the reception and dismission of members, when the quorum shall be the moderator and two members of the session. The session may fix its own quorum at any higher number" (G-10.0202).

To ensure that membership on the session is truly representative, the Form of Government provides two safeguards: a rotating system of active service for elders and a requirement that the session include in its minutes annually a statement of how its membership is inclusive of the diversity of the congregation. Those churches whose membership is limited and who therefore experience difficulty in providing rotation of terms for their officers may request presbytery for a waiver of this requirement. Such exemption from the requirement may be granted for not more than three years at a time and is subject to renewal or revocation at any time by a majority vote of the presbytery.

The Form of Government requires that there always be three classes of elders on the session and three classes of deacons on the board of deacons. These classes shall be as nearly equal in number as possible, and the term of only one class shall expire each year. "No elder or deacon shall be elected for a term of more than three years, nor shall an elder or deacon serve for consecutive terms, either full or partial, aggregating more than six years" (G-14.0201a). Terms shall ordinarily be for three years. A congregation may declare a time of ineligibility after one term. Elders and deacons are nominated by a representative nominating committee whose task it shall be to ensure adequate representation on the boards (G-14.0201b). Exemptions from these requirements are spelled out in the *Book of Order* and will remain in effect until 1998.

The pastor of the church is the moderator of the session. In churches where there are co-pastors, they shall, when present, alternately preside. However, there may be occasions when it is prudent for the pastor not to moderate the session. In such cases the pastor, with the concurrence of the session, may invite some other minister of the Word to preside. If the pastor is ill or absent, the same expedient may be adopted, or, after having gained the approval of the pastor, the session may convene and elect one of its own members to preside. The sessions of vacant churches (those without an installed pastor) are moderated by a minister of the Word appointed by the presbytery. On particular occasions the session may invite another minister from the same presbytery to preside.

One of the compelling reasons for these regulations is that they preserve the unity and interconnected nature of the governing bodies of the Presbyterian Church. The minister is a member of presbytery and, as such, serves to facilitate the relationship of the congregation with the larger church. At the same time, neither pastor nor session can exercise authority without the other. Together they form, under Christ, the authority necessary to discharge their responsibility for the spiritual government of the congregation.

The pastor may call a meeting of the session whenever he or she deems it necessary and must do so when requested in writing by any two members of the session. The session also meets when directed to do so by the presbytery. In any event, the session is required by the Constitution to hold stated meetings at least quarterly. Members of the congregation may attend meetings of the session at the discretion of that body.

In order that the business of the session shall proceed in an orderly fashion, a docket is usually prepared. This is often done by the clerk, in consultation with the pastor, and should anticipate all matters that need to come before the session. Since the session is charged with maintaining the mission and government of the congregation, various areas of responsibility ought to come regularly before it for prayerful consideration. Proper planning and procedure are necessary if the whole life of the church is to produce a body of Christians "mature in Christ." And since the congregation is an inseparable part of the denomination, the concerns of both local and worldwide mission need due consideration. A docket for a meeting of the session might contain the following items:

1. Opening prayer
2. Taking the roll
3. Reading and approval of the minutes

4. Communications from presbytery, synod, and General Assembly
5. Reports of permanent and special committees
6. Report of the 'pastor(s)
7. Report of the clerk
8. Report of the treasurer
9. Examination and reception of new members and/or dismissal of members
10. Arrangements for the Lord's Supper and baptism when necessary
11. Report to presbytery (when in order)
12. Reports of commissioners to other governing bodies
13. Unfinished business
14. Other new or miscellaneous business
15. Adjournment with prayer and benediction

Following the opening prayer, the first items of business fall to the clerk. The clerk is an elder, elected to the office by the session. The responsibilities of the clerk include keeping an accurate record of attendance, recording the minutes of session meetings and meetings of the congregation, issuing letters of transfer, reporting to other governing bodies as required, transmitting to the session communications from other governing bodies and ecumenical agencies, and supervising and maintaining the required registers of church membership. Keeping the roll of the session means recording both those present and those absent at each meeting. Minutes are read to ensure accuracy, before they are permanently entered into the minute book, and are examined each year by the presbytery.

The docket also indicates reports of permanent and special committees. In a smaller church, the session often acts as a committee of the whole to transact its business, but in most cases there will be work that has been assigned to committees, some of which will have members from the congregation at large as well as from the session. The session cannot do all the work of the church. It should divide, assign, and oversee the total program, in which everyone carries part of the load. But policy and direction are the prerogatives of the session, and committee reports make up a large part of the agenda of a session meeting.

Permanent committees carry responsibility for various phases of the continuing program of the church, while special committees are constituted for a particular task and dissolved when the task is completed. Since no two churches or communities are alike, no single committee structure will work equally well everywhere. The mission of the church is one, but the way in which it is done will vary from place to place and from time to time. Yet every session bears similar responsibilities, and some suggestions may be made about organization that can be adapted by almost any session.

1. The prime responsibility of the session is to assist the pastor in the oversight of the spiritual welfare of the congregation. This shepherding office may well be carried out by the session as a whole. The Form of Government states that "members shall, when encouraged by the session, regularly review and evaluate the integrity with which they are involved in the ministry of the church and consider ways in which their participation in the worship and service of the church may be increased and made more meaningful" (G-5.0501). The church is more than a congregation of individuals. By precept and example the session must seek to achieve an organism in which every member finds meaning and usefulness in relation to the whole and matures in the life of prayer and the spirit.

In a smaller congregation where "everybody knows everybody," the care of the congregation may be relatively simple: new members will be made welcome, the sick will be visited, friendship encouraged among the people, family and personal crises met with loving support. In an urban church or a large congregation, care of the members will be a heavier responsibility and will require intentional organization to achieve. The parish may be divided into geographical sections, with elders and deacons assigned the responsibility to encourage and develop teams of members who will report removals from the community, visit in cases of illness or need, help assimilate new members, arrange for home meetings for prayer and study, and otherwise provide for Christian fellowship among members. This is an invaluable service to pastors, who cannot maintain this sort of relationship with a large membership. The pastors in their own visiting can be informed by elders of those needing pastoral care.

2. The session has the responsibility and power "to provide for the worship of the people of God, including the preaching of the Word, the sharing of the Sacraments, and for the music program, in keeping with the principles in the Directory for the Service of God" (G-10.0102c). Worship is the very heart of the Christian community, the one indispensable function of the people of God. It is therefore a primary duty of the session not only to provide occasions for worship but to persuade the people of its importance and encourage them in regular attendance. While the elders may properly expect that the minister of the Word is best qualified to lead congregational worship, it is by no means his or her responsibility alone. Pastors will seek the counsel and support of the session in planning to carry out this aspect of the church's ministry. There should be a

committee on worship to which other members of the congregation may be co-opted. This committee will work with the pastor(s) and the professional musicians, if any, in all aspects of the church's worship: the music program, choosing and training ushers, the schedule and preparation for the sacraments, the order and times of worship, and provision for filling the pulpit in the absence of the pastor. Training in the art of worship, in order that persons of all ages may participate meaningfully, is also a concern of the session.

3. The Christian education program of the church is also under the supervision of the session. The Form of Government refers to its duty "to provide for the growth of its members and for their equipment for ministry through personal and pastoral care, educational programs including the church school, sharing in fellowship and mutual support, and opportunities for witness and service in the world" and "to develop and supervise the church school and the educational program of the church" (G-10.0102d–e). The church is a community of learners seeking to discern the movement of faith and the meaning of ministry. Membership is composed of persons of all ages and may include persons with handicapping conditions and persons of various ethnic and cultural backgrounds. Christian nurture must encompass spiritual growth and knowledge of Christian history and heritage, the content and teaching of the Bible, and the development of the ability to make ethical decisions and to work for the kingdom's goals of justice and peace for all humankind.

A Christian education committee will help the session to plan and carry out the responsibility for the varied aspects of the church's educational ministry. Among the duties of the committee will be leadership recruitment and training; recommending and planning educational programs for all ages, including youth and young adult programs; concerns for the aging and those with special needs; family life emphases; stewardship education; an understanding of and commitment to the global mission of the church; preparation for study, reflection, and action in the community and beyond on issues facing the Christian in the world; recommendations for educational materials; and the coordination of the educational program of the congregation with its worship and service. An enthusiastic and well-informed committee can transform the character of the church and its ministry.

4. The session will also be concerned with the finances of the church. It will "challenge the people of God with the privilege of responsible Christian stewardship of money and time and talents, developing effective ways for encouraging and gathering the offerings of the people and assuring that all offerings are distributed to the objects toward which they were contributed" and will "establish the annual budget, determine the distribution of the church's benevolences, and order offerings for Christian purposes, providing full information to the congregation of its decisions in such matters" (G-10.0102g–h). This responsibility may be handled in a variety of ways. A finance committee of the session may be formed, especially in those churches that do not have trustees. In those instances where a board of trustees exists, the session must nevertheless supervise their work. A joint committee may facilitate this task. In any case, the session cannot delegate its responsibility for the benevolences of the congregation. A committee on benevolence may perform several duties: studying and informing the congregation of the benevolence needs of the General Assembly and other governing

bodies; proposing the share of financial support that the congregation will contribute; providing programs of education and information in order that the congregation may respond intelligently and generously. The distinction sometimes made about the budget of the church where some portions are designated as "for ourselves" and other portions "for others" is a doubtful one. We are a world church and our mission is one mission, whether carried out locally, nationally, or worldwide. The committee may seek the help of presbytery and of ecumenical agencies as it seeks to enable the congregation to be faithful to the unity of the church and to its obligation to the larger fellowship of which it is a part.

The committees just mentioned are merely suggestions. Sessions may function effectively with more or fewer or different ones. In some churches the evangelistic effort is assigned to a committee; in others stewardship is made a special assignment, as is care of the property. Flexibility of organization is necessary if all situations are to be met and the needs of the congregation and the church at large are properly considered. What we have suggested here gives an indication of how an elder may serve as a member of the session. Elders will have responsibilities beyond serving on a committee or committees. These are spelled out in some detail in the Form of Government (G-10.0102). An understanding of the nature and mission of the church is necessary, and learning about these will be a part of the continuing education of the elders. Regular occasions for study and discussion of a wide range of topics related to the responsibilities of the elder should be part of the ongoing work of the session.

The church believes that the will of God is revealed through the Holy Spirit in groups of Christians who thoughtfully and prayerfully wait upon God for guidance. The session meeting should, therefore, provide for more than the business of the church; it should provide opportunity for spiritual growth of its members through worship and study. The elders should be growing into the maturity that is in Christ. The Presbyterian Church (U.S.A.) is convinced that it can go no faster and no further than the vision and knowledge of its officers will permit. It has provided in its Constitution "to engage in a process for education and mutual growth of the members of the session" (G-10.0102j). With the educational agencies of the General Assembly there have been provided materials for preparing elders for their responsibilities and personal growth, both before their ordination and on a continuing basis. Thus elders may enlarge their insights into the nature of the church, deepen their loyalty to Christ by a clearer discernment of Jesus' meanings for personal faith and the world's salvation, and become more effective and enthusiastic workers as they see their part in the whole structure and program of the church.

V
The Churches and the Church

When we think about organized Christianity (and has there ever been any other kind?), many of us will at once picture the particular church with which we are most familiar, probably the one to which we belong. We know it as a relatively small religious community carrying on its varied activities and often seeming to be complete in and of itself. It is busy in a full life of worship, fellowship, teaching, and service which have come to have value and meaning to members through their participation. To all intents and purposes it may appear autonomous in regulating its own affairs and in owning and maintaining its property. Some denominations, which are "congregational" in form of government, define the overall church as precisely all these individual churches entering voluntarily into cooperation with each other, without, however, involving any curtailment of the sovereignty which adheres by right in each congregation.

The Presbyterian idea is quite different. The local congregation is understood as a member within the organism which is the total church. Presbyterian churches are not independent and autonomous; each is related essentially and structurally to the larger body of which it is indissolubly a part. The Presbyterian Church and the churches are mutually involved in such a way that neither can exist without the other: one church, indivisible and universal, must exist in the churches; but it is the faith vitally experienced in the churches which gives reality and power to the church. The Form of Government states "that the several different congregations of believers, taken collectively, constitute one Church of Christ, called emphatically the Church . . ." (G-1.0400). This may seem confusing at first, but it is the basic principle of Presbyterian government and discipline. The local congregation, although given a great deal of freedom in the determination of its affairs, is not autonomous. The Constitution provides that this freedom is exercised within well-defined limits. A congregation cannot by itself call and install its choice of a pastor; it is the prerogative of the presbytery to participate in the search and to approve the call and install the pastor. Ministers of the Word hold membership in presbytery and not in the local church. The minutes of the session must be presented for examination to the presbytery, and all decisions and actions of the session and congregation may be reviewed by the presbytery. Presbytery has the ecclesiastical power to discipline a church, its session or its pastor.

The Presbyterian Church is essentially one body, for we have one *Book of Confessions,* one Constitution and Form of Government, and one common program as defined by the whole church through its General Assembly. In reality, we are a close-knit unity.

This unity is expressed through a representative form of government. Each congregation, through its session, is represented in the presbytery by a commissioner or commissioners. In turn, on a ratio basis and by a balanced number of elders and ministers of the Word, each presbytery elects representatives to attend the General Assembly. This is the most inclusive governing body of our denomination, with jurisdiction extending over the entire church. This system of government should not seem strange to us in the United States, for in many respects there is a remarkable parallel between our civil government and that of our church. Local units of government—towns, counties, and states— approximate congregations and presbyteries; and the federal government, functioning through legislative, administrative, and judicial branches, approximates the General Assembly with its various agencies and units. This form of government expresses the unity and solidarity of the whole yet makes ample room for local independence and initiative. How does this affect the elder who serves in the session of a local church?

We have seen that the session is responsible for the benevolence program of the congregation. Every congregation that is worthy of the name of a Christian church should be doing something for others. It is a service agency carrying out the will of Christ. Its areas of concern are not limited to its own life but extend to the surrounding community and to the wider needs of the nation and the world. No church that is not growing in the range of its vision and outreach will increase spiritual vitality within itself. Encouraging the church in obedience to its Lord to undertake tasks beyond its own walls and to propose ways and means by which this may be accomplished can be the most exciting and stimulating aspect of the work of an elder.

A notable New Testament scholar, speaking of the mission of the church, has said that its life and work should be a continuation of that which Jesus began to do in his short ministry on earth. In fact, when we understand the church truly, it is itself a manifestation in the world of the present activity of the living Christ working through the

Holy Spirit. The Gospels make it clear that Jesus conceived his work to be to preach the gospel of God, to teach the meaning of that gospel in relation to life, and to use his Spirit-given power to heal and help the needy. The church has always understood its mission in terms which it believed Christ had commissioned: "Go therefore and make disciples of all nations . . . teaching them to observe all that I have commanded you; and lo, I am with you always, to the end of the age" (Matt. 28:19–20). The God-given tasks of the church are thus to include evangelism, teaching, and service in the name of Christ.

To this end the General Assembly has created various agencies, responsible to it, which plan and administer programs for the whole church and which aid the congregations and governing bodies together to carry out the one mission of the church. Among these agencies are those whose major responsibility is for programs and ministries of education and nurture. Study courses for children, youth, and adults are prepared for the church. The development of leaders, including teachers, pastors, educators, and officers, is assisted through strategies, programs, support, and materials fashioned in cooperation with governing bodies. Conferences are supported for various groups in the church. Cooperation with colleges, universities, and seminaries helps to ensure their support and the continuation of high standards of academic and religious achievement. In short, wherever there is an evident need for teaching in any part of the church, the services of its agencies of education are called upon.

To meet the challenge of making disciples, both at home and around the globe, the General Assembly, in cooperation with other governing bodies and ecumenical institutions, supports and encourages programs of evangelism. To make Jesus Christ known to the world's people is a constant concern. Where there exist cooperative bodies, such as councils of churches, cooperation makes possible a united approach to common problems. The unity of the church of Jesus Christ compels Presbyterians to work with others of like mind and concern in efforts to witness to the gospel through word and deed.

Other ministries related to the General Assembly assist the church in its outreach to those in need at home and abroad. Schools, hospitals, agriculture programs, health, justice, and education are concerns that, along with telling the good news, accompany our mission efforts. Starting new churches as well as redeveloping those that have fallen on hard times is a part of the outreach of the church through General Assembly action. Because of our deep commitment to the diversity of the church in its unity, the Assembly provides leadership, funding, programs, and resources that make the enrichment of the total church possible through the contributions of those of differing racial and ethnic origins. The church speaks in a variety of tongues, and the mosaic of its life is full of the colors of all of God's races.

The work of the church is one work. The U.S. church receives mission endeavors from other countries and seeks to learn more about its life and work from those sent to us by other churches. Fraternal workers from the worldwide church bring new opportunities for ministry and mission to churches in every part of the world. Further, the Presbyterian Church contributes to world Christianity through active participation in such alliances as the World Council of Churches and the World Alliance of Reformed Churches. Well-developed programs of global and ecumenical education are needed in each local church. The General Assembly agencies provide information and often make available the services of missionary personnel.

Nor does the church forget its servants who have labored long and faithfully in its service. Pension systems have been devised to provide retirement income for church workers and to offer emergency assistance in many areas such as health and education. Homes for the aged and relief for widows are also part of the church's pension system.

Other areas of concern addressed at the General Assembly level include theological education and relationships with the seminaries of the denomination; the development of worship and liturgical aids and education; keeping the church informed about social issues and recommending action to ease social, economic, and justice ills; racial and ethnic concerns; and programs for women and men in the church.

The persons who make up these agencies are elected by the General Assembly from congregations and governing bodies across the church. They are created by the General Assembly—that is, by women and men from local congregations who gather as the Assembly—and through prayerful consideration of the life of the church and the issues facing it, and led by the Holy Spirit they make decisions about program, budget, priorities, and directions. The agencies are not autonomous; they report to the General Assembly and their policies are determined by Assembly-elected boards. They are staffed by dedicated women and men who consider their work as a ministry to which God has called them and in which they serve as do all servants of Jesus Christ.

This has been a very rapid review of the Presbyterian way of responding to the commission of Christ. At every level, elders may be called upon to render service. Elders should consider service rendered to governing bodies beyond the session as a joyous opportunity to serve the church of Christ. Meetings of presbytery and other governing bodies are places where the ministry of the church is debated and implemented. Presbyters (elders and ministers of the Word) are part of the governance of a denomination that is not sectarian in its point of view—that is, it does not hold a narrow or exclusivist concept of the Christian faith but is true to the broad spirit and to the ancient and modern creeds of the world church. Presbyterians are eager to unite with other Christians in promoting the essential unity of the church of Christ. It is our prayer that all may be one, in spirit and witness if not in name, even as Christ desired, together bringing healing, peace, and unity to a broken world. Elders are privileged to witness and serve in such a church.

VI
The Session
and the Pastor

"And from Miletus he sent to Ephesus and called to him the elders of the church" (Acts 20:17). The strong bond of fellowship between the elders in the church at Ephesus and the apostle Paul reminds us of the unique relation between the session and the pastor. The parallel is not exact, for the apostle was not a settled minister in a parish. Yet on the occasion of a prolonged visit to the city during the course of a missionary journey, he doubtless had opportunity for extended collaboration, from which grew the mutual esteem and love so movingly depicted in the incident described by Luke. There is no other enterprise in the world in which persons are so drawn to one another and to the leader as in the labor that elders and pastors undertake for their Lord and Savior. Friendship naturally develops where persons are thrown together in common endeavors, and it may be unusually firm under special circumstances. But the fraternity of pastor and elders is based on the communion that Christ creates by his Spirit. It was described by Jesus, when he said to his disciples:

> You are my friends if you do what I command you. No longer do I call you servants, for the servant does not know what his master is doing; but I have called you friends, for all that I have heard from my Father I have made known to you. You

did not choose me, but I chose you and appointed you that you should go and bear fruit and that your fruit should abide; so that whatever you ask the Father in my name, he may give it to you. This I command you, to love one another.

(John 15:14–17)

There are unhappy exceptions to the rule, as might be expected among persons who are far from perfect; but rare is the situation in which a minister does not refer to the elders with pride and affection; conversely, elders speak of their pastor in equally warm terms.

The spirit of mutual regard and unity is not something that "just happens." It must be cultivated. A few suggestions may be helpful in achieving this end.

1. As an expression of Christian principle, the adage "Good fences make good neighbors" leaves much to be desired. Yet it does point to the truth that each of two parties must know and honor mutual rights and privileges if good relations are to be maintained. While it is a technical point, both ministers and elders should know the limits of their respective authority and should not intrude upon spheres assigned to others. For example, some tasks a minister shares equally with elders. Indeed, in the exercise of spiritual rule in the church, ministers and elders are both called presbyters. As presbyters the minister and the elder share equal authority; their votes count the same in presbytery and other governing bodies. This parity is further emphasized by the fact that minister and elders comprise the session and no action taken by either unilaterally is officially valid. But in other ways a minister stands in a unique relationship, both to the session and to the congregation. The minister is a member of the presbytery and not the congregation in which he or she serves. Further, the minister is installed in the church by the

presbytery, to which is reserved the power to remove him or her from it. Changes in the salary of the minister must be approved by presbytery. Thus it is evident that neither the session nor the congregation exercises authority over the minister. It ought also to be understood that the authority of the minister in the church does not rest in the person. In the Presbyterian order of church government, the presbytery exercises the office of bishop, with oversight of each congregation, and the minister is really the representative of presbytery, commissioned to serve a particular congregation. This status gives the minister considerable freedom, which under the authority of presbytery is used to preach the gospel in its purity and fullness and in love. A mutual respect for those provisions of the Form of Government will make for the "good neighborliness" which is so great a blessing.

2. The observations that have just been made are not intended to imply that the session, or an individual elder, should not consult with the minister about any matter concerning the church. Indeed, if the minister is wise, the wisdom and guidance of the officers will be welcome and sought. Every minister can recall with gratitude instances where the sage counsel of an experienced Christian colleague has prevented a rash act, secured balance in judgment, or brought perspective in a confused situation. In helpful ways the session can be the line of communication between pastor and people. Who knows the congregation better than those elected by it? The session should have the concern and the courage to interpret the needs of the people to the minister as it sees them, and the attitude of the minister should be so receptive that such observations will never be construed as reproaches. On the other hand, who has better opportunity to know the minister than

those with whom the office of elder is shared? There often will be times when elders may interpret to the people the hopes, dreams, anxieties, and points of view of the minister. When it may be impossible or unseemly for the minister to speak for herself or himself, members of the session who love and trust their minister can effectively speak out. This mutual confidence and reciprocity is both the fruit of the Spirit's work and the condition of the Spirit's further operation. This is in large measure the secret of the fellowship of kindred minds.

3. No minister who is sensitive to the proprieties of the call and who is unselfish in motive will divulge to the session or the congregation the happiness that a little thoughtfulness on their part would bring to the minister and the minister's family. While the minister and members of his or her family are constantly with people, theirs is often a lonely task. The pastor bears the burdens of the flock, and the people may never know their weight. The minister and the minister's family have needs and emergencies, and elders are in a better position than anyone else to know what these needs and burdens are. It is their privilege to help, individually as friends and collectively as the session. No minister deliberately and openly seeks tokens of the people's appreciation and affection, yet ministers are human and need the warmth of personal friendships which professional relationships cannot bring.

4. At each celebration of the Lord's Supper our memory is stirred by reflection upon the presence of the Lord and the disciples at the Last Supper. This reflection is especially meaningful to ministers and elders who unite in the performance of this sacrament. Even as the disciples in the upper room enjoyed a profound comradeship, so it is no presumption for ministers and elders to seek the same at the Table. The Communion table is placed so that the

family of faith may gather about it. The minister officiates in the name of the unseen Lord, whose presence is no less real because it is "in the spirit." The minister gives the elements to those who serve with him or her in the care of the people of God, who then distribute them to the gathered worshipers, as Jesus blessed, broke, and gave the bread through his disciples to the multitude. The unity in Christ between minister and elders is typified by their service at the Table. It is here that minister and elders dedicate themselves to serve the congregation. There is order, division of responsibility, and a recognition of the value of the labors of each.

All that has been written in this book is based on the premise that to serve as elder in the Presbyterian Church is an honor and a rewarding service. It is not the sort of honor desired by the world, where one receives praise and plaudits; rather, it is the satisfaction that comes when one is called by the Spirit through the voice of the church to serve Jesus Christ. The secret of effectiveness as an elder will be dependence on God, a wholehearted commitment to one's responsibilities, and continuing growth. As elders join in conferences and training experiences intended to promote the development of their gifts, as they sincerely study the will of God for their own lives and usefulness, as they faithfully carry out their duties to the people whose spiritual welfare is their concern, they will gain a sense of worth and enduring satisfaction. This is service which requires much and pays large dividends. May God bless all who are called to it.